Habitats

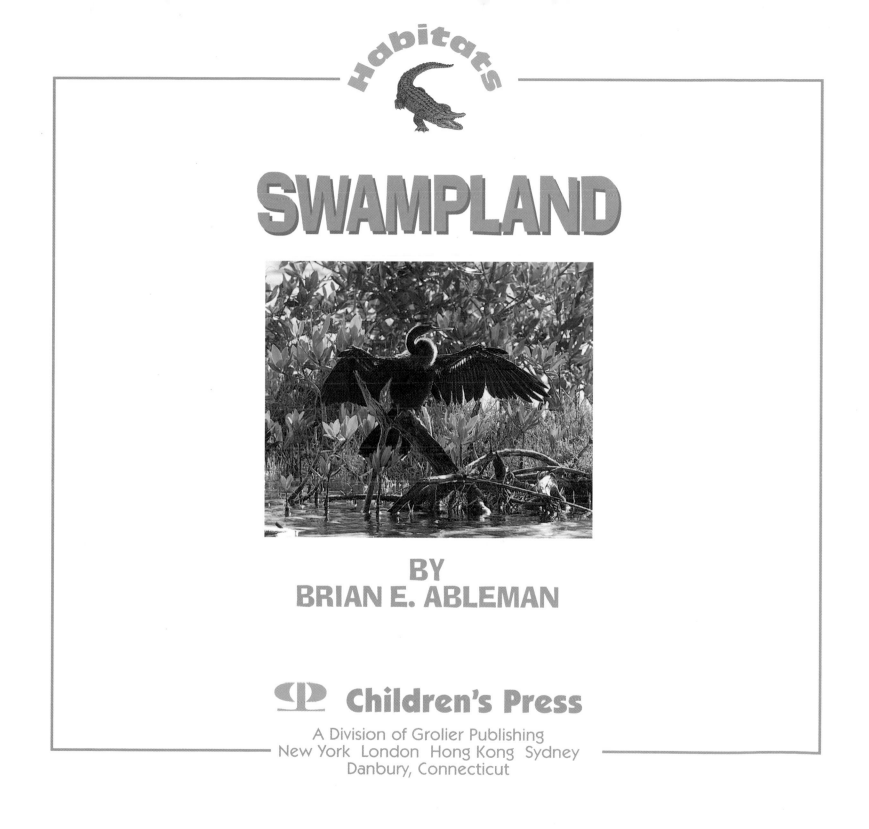

SWAMPLAND

BY
BRIAN E. ABLEMAN

Children's Press

A Division of Grolier Publishing
New York London Hong Kong Sydney
Danbury, Connecticut

Created and Developed by The Learning Source

Designed by Josh Simons

All illustrations by Glenn Quist

Photo Credits: David M. Dennis/ Tom Stack & Associates: 10 (right bottom); Richard B. Dippold/Unicorn Stock Photos: 27; Kerry T. Givens/Tom Stack: 7; Jeff Greenberg/Unicorn: 20-21; Bernard Hehl/Unicorn: 1; Judy Hile/Unicorn: 11; Tom & Pat Leeson: 28 (left); Joe McDonald/Tom Stack: 10 (right top), 12, 13 (left), 18; Margo Moss/Unicorn: 8 (left), 28 (right), back cover; Brian Parker/Tom Stack: 19; Fred Reischl/Unicorn: 4-5, 15 (top), 17; John Shaw/Tom Stack: front cover; Tom Stack/Tom Stack: 9, 29; SuperStock, Inc.: 10 (left), 23; Lynn M. Stone: 2, 6, 8 (right), 13 (right), 14, 15 (bottom), 22, 25, 26, 32.

Library of Congress Cataloging-in-Publication Data
Ableman, Brian E.
    Swampland / by Brian E. Ableman.
      p. cm. — (Habitats)
    Summary: Describes the characteristics of the Okefenokee Swamp and the animals that live there.
    ISBN 0-516-20743-1 (lib. bdg.)   0-516-20374-6 (pbk.)
    1. Swamp animals—Okefenokee Swamp (Ga. and Fla.)—Juvenile literature. 2. Swamp ecology—Okefenokee Swamp (Ga. and Fla.)—Juvenile literature. [1. Swamp animals. 2. Swamp ecology. 3. Ecology. 4. Okefenokee Swamp (Ga. and Fla.)] I. Title. II. Series: Habitats (Children's Press)
QL 114.A25   1997
591.768'09758'752—dc21   97-26986   CIP
                                              AC

Printed in the United States of America
1 2 3 4 5 6 7 8 9 10 R 06 05 04 03 02 01 00 99 98 97

Tucked away in the southeastern corner of the United States, nearly forgotten, lies an ancient, watery world called Okefenokee (oh kee fen OH kee). It is a swamp, a squishy place where the air and land are almost as dark and wet as the water.

It is dawn now in the Okefenokee, but only a stray sunbeam or two ever reach the ground. A thick overgrowth of trees, shrubs, and bushes screens out most of the light.

mosquito

  As the sun comes up, the air buzzes with the sound
of insect wings. Gnats so small that they are almost
invisible swarm in the trees. Katydids feed on tender
leaves while dragonflies grow fat as they gobble up
mosquito after mosquito.

In this soggy place the plants, too, can be fierce. A spider stops to rest on a leaf. It snoops around the plant until, in a flash, it topples down a tube and disappears forever. The spider has become a tasty meal for the insect-eating pitcher plant.

Cypress trees like these stretch 120 feet (36.6 meters) up into the sky. As they struggle to reach their own patch of sunlight, the trees twist into strange shapes that look like knees and legs and arms.

In spite of its name, Spanish moss is not really moss at all. It actually is an organism called an epiphyte (EP ah fight). Spanish moss gets its food from the air and rainwater. Scaly hairs on the stems give the plant its gray color.

Hanging from the limbs of cypress trees are long, hairy clumps of Spanish moss. In the flickering light, the moss-covered trees seem to turn into spooky ghosts and goblins.

Frogs are everywhere. So are salamanders. They hop, scurry, and hide, doing whatever they can to escape all the hungry predators around them.

A giant snapping turtle has a wiggly growth on its tongue. The turtle shakes this growth from side to side. Passing fish sometimes mistake it for a swimming worm and end up as the turtle's dinner.

Turtles roam the land and the water. Small ones use their shells as protection from enemies. But giant snapping turtles, which can weigh as much as 150 pounds (67.5 kilograms), have little to fear.

Many kinds of snakes slither through the water,
trees, and grass. Some, like this water snake, can only
do harm to creatures smaller or slower than they are.

Other snakes, such as this poisonous cottonmouth, are dangerous to almost everything. A cottonmouth will swim or hang almost unseen from a tree limb. Then, without warning, it will attack some unsuspecting animal.

The absolute ruler of the swamp is the mighty alligator. As an adult, it often grows to 15 feet (4.6 meters) of muscle, scaly hide, and big teeth. An alligator will eat almost anything, even another alligator.

When the weather grows cool, an alligator's digestive system slows down almost to a stop. This leaves the alligator feeling so full that even turtles can sit safely nearby.

By day, an alligator usually rests, sunning itself or floating, like a log, in the water. But by night the alligator hunts, feasting on frogs, turtles, or even birds and small mammals.

A female alligator makes a nest by piling up plants and roots. Then she wiggles her body on the pile to make a deep hole for her eggs. There the eggs can stay, safe and warm, until they are ready to hatch.

After they leave their shells, baby alligators are closely watched by their mother. Slowly, the youngsters learn the ways of the swamp. In time they will be off on their own.

If the eggs in an alligator nest become too cool, only females will hatch. Only males will hatch if the eggs are too warm. To make an even balance of males and females, the mother alligator uses her body to control the temperature in the nest.

Otters and other mammals hunt or fish in the swamp.
But they are always on guard, alert to the dangers
around them.

In most habitats on earth, mammals usually rule. In the
swamp, however, reptiles seem to have the upper hand.

Yet, the mammals continue to come. Raccoons seek places to hunt. Opossums, such as this one, find homes wherever they can.

Close by, in the shallow waters of the swamp, a pine-covered island rises. Here, some larger mammals can sometimes find a comfortable home. This little fawn, for instance, lives well, nibbling on the island's plentiful supply of shrubs and trees.

Bobcats, too, roam among the pines. Fast and deadly predators, these fierce wildcats hunt whatever they please. Young deer and wild pigs must be especially careful to stay out of their way.

At one time, magnificent Florida panthers were common in the swamp. Now it is rare to see one on the island or anywhere else in the Okefenokee.

The largest mammals in the swamp are black bears. Like this fellow, they are often seen lumbering through bushes or clambering up trees in search of tasty bugs.

The voice of the swamp definitely belongs to the birds and insects. Any time of day, an orchestra of cheeps, caws, and buzzes can be heard. Small birds, such as mocking birds and redwing blackbirds, live in shrubs and trees. Here, it is very easy to find noisy insects and juicy berries to eat.

Large sandhill cranes wade into the shallow swamp water, looking for food. They poke around, using their long beaks to catch tasty fish that swim by.

This bird's bill is like a great shovel. Standing in shallow water, it moves its bill back and forth. When the bill touches something, it snaps shut, trapping the bird's meal inside.

Here, too, the roseate spoonbill makes its home.
Fifty years ago this red-feathered bird was nearly extinct.
Now, there are more than 1,000 nesting pairs alive.

Nearby, an anhinga swims at top speed to trap and eat a frog. Then the water-soaked bird comes ashore to dry out. Unlike most birds, anhingas do not have a waxy coating on their wings. So instead of sliding off, water soaks through the birds' feathers, leaving it no choice but to hang out to dry.

As night falls, herons return home with food for their hungry chicks. Most of the birds will sleep now. But for some mammals, insects, and reptiles night is the time to hunt. After floating all day in the water, this alligator is looking for a big meal.

The setting sun brings with it the buzzing of insects and the squishing and splashing of hungry animals on the prowl. Here in the swamp, life continues as it has for thousands of years, untouched, except for the water, the weather, and the creatures that call it home.

More About

Anhinga, Page 1:
The anhinga is also known as a "darter." The name comes from the way these birds use their long necks and sharp-pointed bills to spear, or dart, fish.

Frogs, Page 10:
Most frogs actually can jump as much as 20 times their own body lengths. Measure out 20 times your body length and see if you can jump that far!

The Everglades, Pages 4-5:
The Everglades is a swamp more than four times the size of the Okefenokee. It covers more than 2,746 square miles (7,112 square kilometers) of southern Florida.

Salamander, Page 10:
If a salamander gets a leg or tail caught or bitten off, it has nothing to worry about. Salamanders have the amazing ability to grow new limbs to replace ones that are lost!

Spider, Page 7:
A spider's web is so strong that even insects much bigger and stronger than spiders cannot escape from it.

Snapping Turtle, Page 11:
Most turtles have large shells to protect them from enemies. But not the snapping turtle. Its shell is so small that it depends on its strong jaws for defense.

This Habitat

Snake, Page 12:
Snakes use their teeth for capturing prey, not eating it. They open their big, stretchable jaws and swallow their prey whole— while it is still alive.

Opossum, Page 19:
Opossums are related to kangaroos and other animals that carry their young in pouches. Opossums also have 50 teeth, more than any other mammal in North America!

Alligator, Page 14:
Alligators and crocodiles are related and can be difficult to tell apart. But crocodiles have a more pointed snout. They also weigh less and grow more quickly.

Florida Panther, Page 22:
This rare animal actually is a mountain lion. It is such an excellent jumper that it often pounces on its prey from high up on the limb of a tree.

Otter, Page 18:
Otters are such expert swimmers that they can stay under water for up to four minutes at a time. They even have ears and nostrils that close in order to keep out water.

Sandhill Crane, Page 25:
Nearly five feet (1.52 meters) tall, sandhill cranes are able to see over the tall grasses and bushes of the swamp. Their loud cry, like a bugle call, warns creatures of coming danger.

Usborne

Big Picture Book
Dinosaurs

Laura Cowan

Illustrated by Gianluca Foli

Designed by Zoe Wray

Expert: Dr. Darren Naish, University of Southampton

Usborne Quicklinks

For links to websites where you can watch video clips
about dinosaurs and learn how to say all the names in this book, go to

www.usborne.com/quicklinks and type in the keywords, 'big picture dinosaurs'.

We recommend that children are supervised while using the internet.
Please follow the internet safety guidelines at the Usborne Quicklinks website.

Contents

Each big picture scene in this book shows dinosaurs
that lived together during the same period.

Hello, dinosaurs!

Millions and millions of years ago, long before there were people, the world belonged to creatures unlike any you've ever seen. Many of these were DINOSAURS. Millions of years is SUCH a long time, it's hard to imagine. But try.

At first, there was NOTHING living on Earth. No plants. No animals. Just rocks.

POP

From the nothing, slowly, slowly, over millions and millions and MILLIONS of years, living things grew.

SPLOSH

SPLAT

TIKTAALIK

JELLYFISH

DIMETRODON

The names of animals that are NOT DINOSAURS are shown like this.

About 200 million years ago, the first types of dinosaurs appeared.

Hello, dinosaur!

There were plants, such as ferns, but no flowers.

COELOPHYSIS

The names of different types of dinosaur are shown like this.

4

Most of the first dinosaurs were only the size of a big dog or a cow. But later dinosaurs came in all different shapes and sizes.

ARRRRP

Some were **feathery** and some were **furry**. Some were **scaly**, too.

Some had **big** heads, some had big tails, and some had **jagged teeth** and **sharp claws**.

Some were tiny but some were **BIGGER** than **ANY** animal **EVER** to walk the earth.

STAURIKOSAURUS

This was the world of the dinosaurs.

RIOJASAURUS

These gentle giants lived together peacefully – there was lots of food for everyone.

DIPLODOCUS

Gentle giants

Lots of dinosaurs were big and slow. These kinds only ate plants, but still grew as big as a BUS or a HOUSE. They plodded around in groups called herds.

ORNITHOLESTES

CAMPTOSAURUS

Ornitholestes was not like the giant dinosaurs. It ate MEAT.

LOOK OUT, CAMPTOSAURUS – Ornitholestes wants to eat you!

NIP, NIP!

Stumpy front legs for crouching close to the plants it ate

Strong back legs for running

BRONTOSAURUS

Long neck to reach
high up for food

Swoosh!
Swoosh!

When the dinosaurs had eaten
all the food in one place, they
would move to another.

Bony plates stopped
other dinosaurs from
eating Stegosaurus.

THWACK
THWACK

Spiked tail for
swiping at enemies
or annoying
little dinos

STEGOSAURUS

STOP BITING
MY TAIL, TINY
DINOSAUR!

Dinosaur eats dinosaur

Some dinosaurs didn't eat plants and they didn't live in herds. Some dinosaurs were scarier than the rest – they ate OTHER DINOSAURS.

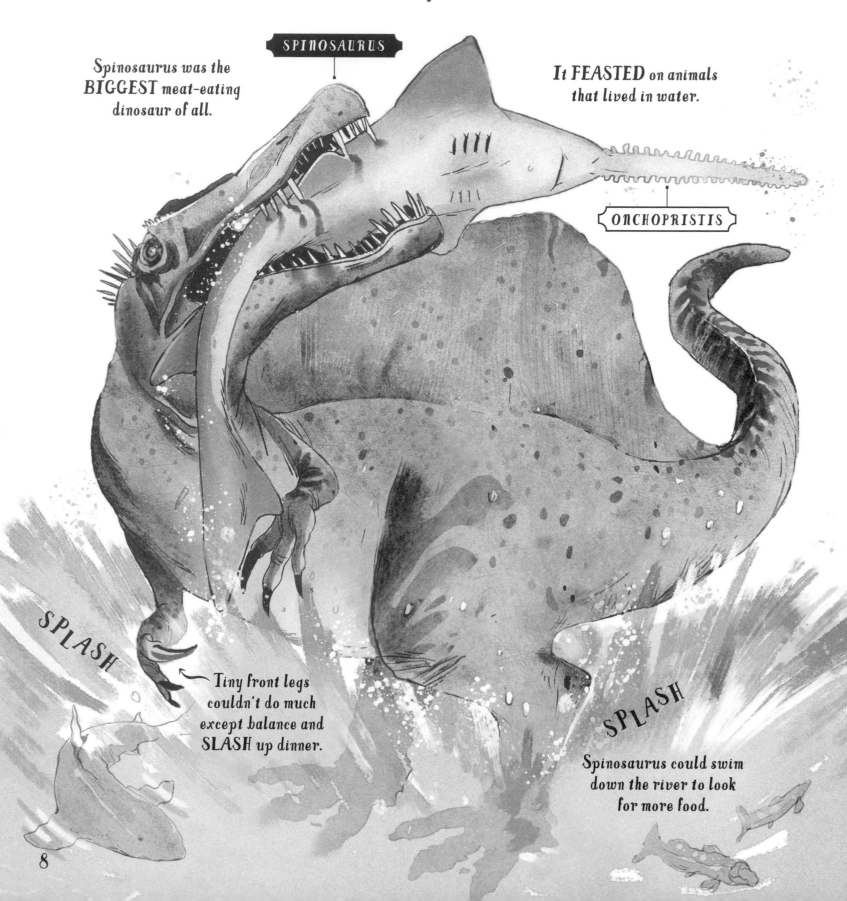

SPINOSAURUS

Spinosaurus was the BIGGEST meat-eating dinosaur of all.

It FEASTED on animals that lived in water.

ONCHOPRISTIS

SPLASH

Tiny front legs couldn't do much except balance and SLASH up dinner.

SPLASH

Spinosaurus could swim down the river to look for more food.

Tyrannosaurus rex – or T.rex for short – was KING of the dinosaurs.
Other dinosaurs were bigger, but T.rex was SCARIER. Other dinosaurs ran away from T.rex.

TYRANNOSAURUS REX

EDMONTOSAURUS

WERGH

Why? Because T.rex ate EVERYTHING. Sometimes it even ate OTHER T.REXES.

This little dinosaur is
nicknamed the 'chicken
from hell' because it looked
like the scariest chicken
EVER.

RAAAAAAAR

ANZU

Uh-oh, is Anzu going to
be GOBBLED UP?

MICRORAPTOR

Tiny dinosaurs

Lots of dinosaurs weren't big at all. They were the size of pigeons. They weren't scary either – some were covered in shiny feathers.

Microraptor used its tail to change direction in the air.

NEOOOOW

Its wings were for gliding and floating on gusts of wind.

Sometimes Microraptor feathers looked black.

Sometimes they shimmered purple, blue and green.

SWOOSH!

IS THAT A BUTTERFLY?

NO, IT ONLY **LOOKS LIKE** A BUTTERFLY.

Kalligramma was an insect that lived over 100 million years ago.

FLITTER FLUTTER

KALLIGRAMMA

Kalligramma flapped its wings and flew up or down or around.

Massive Dinosaur FIGHT!

Argentinosaurus was one of the BIGGEST dinosaurs EVER. Giganotosaurus looked tiny next to Argentinosaurus, but it was HUGE too. And HUNGRY for dinosaur meat...

GIGANOTOSAURUS

SNARL
SNARL

Its teeth weren't good for biting other dinosaurs – they were for chewing plants.

FIGHT!

Giganotosaurus had sharp teeth and claws for slashing – and it fought in packs.

From its nose to the tip of its tail, Argentinosaurus was as long as three buses back to back.

WHOOSH

Argentinosaurus fought back using its **HUGE** tail and **STRONG** legs.

RRRARRRR

SNAP
SNAP

FIGHT!

Could a Giganotosaurus pack take down the biggest dinosaur ever? They're going to try...

PSSSSST! These dinos might not look big next to Argentinosaurus, but look on pages 30-31 and you will see how MASSIVE they really were...

Blending in

Some dinosaurs were very good at hiding – from the animals hunting them... and the things they hunted.

These little dinosaurs were striped like tigers. Stripes helped Sinornithosaurus blend in with the shadows of branches and STRIPES of sunlight.

Sinornithosaurus didn't sleep at night and it didn't sleep in the day. Instead, it had little naps whenever it was tired.

NNNNN

SINORNITHOSAURUS

RRRRR!

THESE INSECTS
WOULD BE A
TASTY MEAL!

BOO!

Sinornithosaurus lurked
in between the trees
where insects couldn't
see it and then...
HELLO, LUNCH!

How many Sinornithosaurus
can you spot?

Standing out

Some dinosaurs were good at hiding, but others did the opposite. They stood out to SCARE AWAY enemies, or to SHOW OFF to friends.

Zhenyuanlong looked like a big bird, but it couldn't fly.

ZHENYUANLONG

Bright feathers said to other male Zhenyuanlongs, GO AWAY, THIS IS MY LAND.

Feathers kept these dinosaurs nice and warm.

Bright feathers on male Zhenyuanlongs said to females, HEY, COME ON OVER.

16

Fanning out tail feathers was a way of showing off to female dinosaurs.

Epidexipteryx also used its tail feathers to help balance on branches.

EPIDEXIPTERYX

OH, HELLO HELLO!

Epidexipteryx was SMALL – just the size of a squirrel. It probably stayed in the trees, to keep safe from the big dinosaurs prowling around down on the ground.

17

Babies

Where did baby dinosaurs come from?
Well, they started life inside
surprisingly small eggs...

MAIASAURA

A female Maiasaura laid 30 or 40 eggs at once.
Each egg was about the size of a big orange.

Maiasaura lined their nests
with leaves and plants to
keep the eggs warm.

A baby dinosaur
grew inside each egg.

When can I
come out of
my shell?

CRRRRRRRRACK

TAP-TAP

Months and
months later,
the shells started
to crack...

18

It was hard being a baby dinosaur. Baby dinosaurs were very small and the world was very big. But Maiasaura lived in herds and they helped each other.

Maiasaura looked after its little babies. It fed them bits of plant, and tried to keep them safe.

PEEP

PEEP

PEEP

PEEP

PEEP

...and babies hatched out of the eggs.

TAP-TAP

PEEP

24-hour desert dinos

Some dinosaurs lived in deserts. Deserts 80 million years ago were like deserts today – except for the dinosaurs.

There's not much to eat in deserts – there aren't as many plants as in other places, just lots of dust. During the daytime, the sun is HOT.

Some dinosaurs dozed during the day. It was too hot for them to move.

PROTOCERATOPS

ZZZZZZ

Other dinosaurs didn't mind heat – they were the ones that moved very... SLOWLY.

PINACOSAURUS

The afternoon was SLEEPY TIME for Protoceratops. Food time was later.

CRRRRUNCH

STOMP

STOMP

STOMP

20

When the sun goes down, the desert cools. Dinosaurs that slept during the day woke up and looked for food at night. For them, it was HUNTING TIME.

Velociraptor and Mononykus had HUGE eyes.

MONONYKUS

HUGE eyes were ALL THE BETTER for seeing things in the dark.

PROTOCERATOPS

REOWWWWWW

VELOCIRAPTOR

WATCH OUT
PROTOCERATOPS!

EEK

Velociraptor could see better and move faster than Protoceratops.

mmmmmMmMMm?

Flight of the pterosaurs

Up in the sky there were **NO** dinosaurs at all. But there were all kinds of amazing flying creatures called pterosaurs.

CROUCH!

VAULT!

TAKE OFF!

TROPEOGNATHUS

Fuzzy hairs called pycnofibres, kept pterosaurs' bodies cosy.

The water had lots of fish – food for pterosaurs.

TAPEJARA

TUPUXUARA

Pterosaurs had light, hollow bones filled with air, so they could float in the sky.

Tupuxuara had a big bony crest on its head. But what was it for?

Letting out heat to keep cool?

Steering through the sky?

So they could show off?

No one knows... yet.

THALASSODROMEUS

Yum yum, delicious baby dinosaurs!

WATCH OUT, PTEROSAURS! CROCODILE ALERT!

SNAP! SNAP!

PTERANODON

STYXOSAURUS

AMMONITE

Sharks might seem huge and dangerous, but these ones were like fluffy kittens compared to STYXOSAURUS.

Sea beasts

Dinosaurs didn't live in the sea either. But there were lots of other creatures that were just as BIG and SCARY as the ones on land.

SQUALICORAX

Goodbye, dinosaurs!

Dinosaurs lived on Earth for more than 150 million years, but they don't any more. What happened to them?

BANG

PEOOOOOW

BOOM

Did lots of volcanoes erupt at once? Spewing ash and soot and molten lava all over the planet?

ROAAAAAAAAAAAAAAAAAAAAAR

WAAAAAAAAAA

Did it get too hot?   Or too cold?

BRRRRRRRR

HU HU
HU HU
HU

Any of these things might have happened.
But then, one day, a rock
AS BIG AS A CITY fell from space.

The ground
shook and broke
into pieces.

Dust shot
into the sky.

WHOOOOOOOOOSH

BOOooom

There was no light,
or warmth. Plants
on the land died.

All the pterosaurs died.
Lots of animals and sea
creatures died.

All the dinosaurs died too –
but they didn't all disappear.
At least, NOT QUITE...

Goodbye forever?

New plants and animals came along.
Millions and millions of years later, people came along, too.
But lots of things are still left from dinosaur times.

These things are called FOSSILS. They are
the traces of living plants or animals
from dinosaur times.

HUGE dinosaur
footprints

This is a fossil of an ammonite.
It lived in the sea in dinosaur times.

Massive
fossil bone

A fossil of a whole nest of dinosaur eggs and the babies inside

More fossils are being found all the time, telling us new things about what dinosaurs were like and how they lived.

This is a feathery tail trapped in AMBER – a liquid from trees that hardens over time. Until VERY recently NO ONE knew dinosaurs had feathers.

This is a tooth that became a fossil made of shiny stone known as opal.

A fossil of a velociraptor skeleton

This looks like a rock, but it's the print of a dinosaur brain in stone.

Did you know that BIRDS are dinosaurs' great great great great great great great great great a million million MILLION greats grandchildren?

So some dinosaurs are STILL HERE...

Who are YOU? You look a little bit like me...

HELLO!

29

BIG
and small

The dinosaurs in this book were all different sizes. Compare them here. How big was little Microraptor? Or ENORMOUS ARGENTINOSAURUS?

TYRANNOSAURUS REX

Roaarrr

Zooooom

TUPUXUARA

Hmmph

ARGENTINOSAURUS

STEGOSAURUS

RIOJASAURUS

MICRORAPTOR

HUMAN

ANZU

BRONTOSAURUS

Grrrrr

COELOPHYSIS

SINORNITHOSAURUS

ZHENYUANLONG

PROTOCERATOPS

GIGANOTOSAURUS

Peep peep

EPIDEXIPTERYX

Snuffle snuffle

MAIASAURA

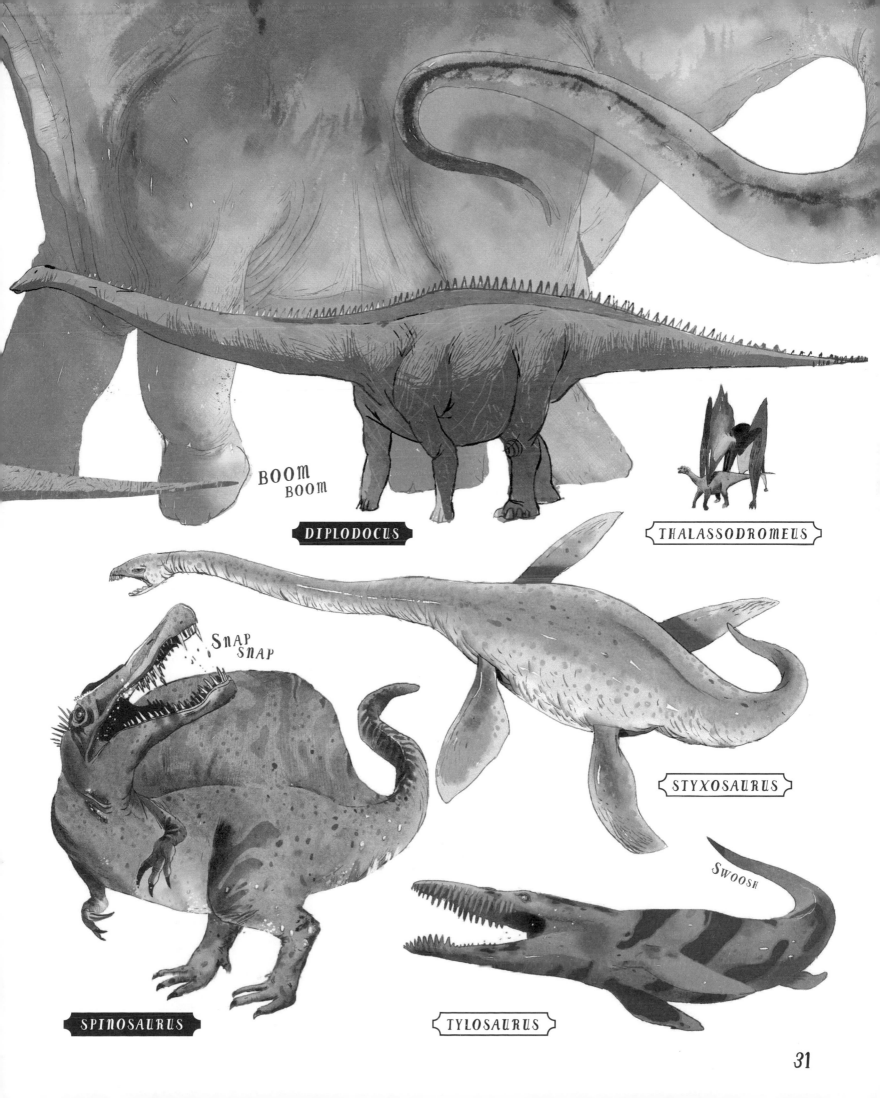

BOOM
BOOM

DIPLODOCUS

THALASSODROMEUS

SNAP
SNAP

STYXOSAURUS

SWOOSH

SPINOSAURUS

TYLOSAURUS

31

Index

Edited by Ruth Brocklehurst
Digital retouching and additional illustration by John Russell